LOUISIANA

Past and Present

Jeri Freedman

rosen publishing's
rosen
central®

New York

Published in 2011 by The Rosen Publishing Group, Inc.
29 East 21st Street, New York, NY 10010

First Edition

Library of Congress Cataloging-in-Publication Data

Freedman, Jeri.
Louisiana : past and present / Jeri Freedman. — 1st ed.
    p. cm. — (The United States: past and present)
Includes bibliographical references and index.
ISBN 978-1-4358-9483-9 (library binding)
ISBN 978-1-4358-9510-2 (pbk. book)
ISBN 978-1-4358-9544-7 (6-pack)
1. Louisiana—Juvenile literature. I. Title.
F369.3.F74 2011
976.3—dc22

2010001616

Manufactured in Malaysia

CPSIA Compliance Information: Batch #CR014001YA: For Further Information Contact Rosen Publishing, New York, New York at 1-800-237-9932

On the cover: Top left: Canal Street, a main thoroughfare in nineteenth-century New Orleans. Top right: Cypress and tupelo trees growing in the Louisiana bayou. Bottom: A 2006 parade celebrating the reopening of Preservation Hall, a historic jazz performance hall in New Orleans's French Quarter.

Contents

Located on the Gulf of Mexico, Louisiana became a state in 1812. Many people flock to Louisiana each year to experience the many things that the state has to offer.

Introduction

Louisiana is located in the center of the southern United States. It is bordered on the south by the Gulf of Mexico, on the west by Texas, on the east by Mississippi, and on the north by Arkansas. Its eastern border is formed by the Mississippi River, and its western border is formed by the Sabine River. The Red River and Ouachita River cross the center of the state. Louisiana is home to a number of lakes, including Lake Pontchartrain in New Orleans and Lake Charles in the southwestern corner of the state.

Louisiana has a population of approximately 4.4 million people. The capital is Baton Rouge, the second largest city in the state, with a population of about 225,000. The largest city in Louisiana is New Orleans, which has a population of three hundred thousand people.

There are many colleges and universities in Louisiana. Among them are Louisiana State University, which has branches at a number of locations; Loyola University and Tulane University in New Orleans; Southern University in Baton Rouge; Nicholls State University in Thibodaux; Louisiana Tech in Ruston; and the University of Louisiana at Lafayette. Louisiana is also home to many historically black colleges and universities, including Dillard University and Xavier University in New Orleans, and Grambling State University in Grambling, Louisiana.

Chapter 1

THE GEOGRAPHY OF LOUISIANA

The state of Louisiana covers 51,843 square miles (134,272.75 square kilometers). Eight thousand two hundred and seventy-seven square miles (21,437 square km) of the state are water. Louisiana is a very low-lying state, located completely within the Gulf Coastal Plain. The state's highest point is Driskill Mountain, which is only 535 feet (165 meters) tall, and the lowest point, New Orleans, is 5 feet (1.5 m) below sea level.

The southern end of Louisiana extends into the Gulf of Mexico. About 125 miles (201 km) from the Gulf, the Mississippi River splits the southeastern tip of Louisiana, forming a crescent-shaped inlet that the river empties into. The city of New Orleans is located here, and the shape of the land on which it sits gives the city the nickname of Crescent City. At the north side of New Orleans is Lake Pontchartrain, which covers 630 square miles (1,630 square km). Lake Pontchartrain is the second largest saltwater lake in the United States, after the Great Salt Lake in Salt Lake City, Utah.

The Geology of Louisiana

Louisiana's land is completely formed by the buildup of sediment deposited by the Mississippi River (and other rivers that existed

Levees protect homes in Kenner, Louisiana. Because much of Louisiana is swampland, the state's inhabitants wage a continual battle to keep floodwaters at bay.

before it) for about fifty million years. Much like now, the seawater from the Gulf of Mexico intermixed with the water from the Mississippi River. This seawater was home to all types of marine life. As these marine animals and plants died, their bodies formed pockets of organic matter under the surface of the water. That matter eventually turned into petroleum.

Over the centuries, floodwater from the Mississippi River continued to deposit sediment at its mouth, building up the surface of the

Hurricanes

Louisiana is located directly off the Gulf of Mexico. As a result, the state is prone to hurricanes. Records of large hurricanes hitting Louisiana stretch back to the eighteenth century. In 1740, a hurricane that hit colonial Louisiana destroyed a large number of crops. These crops had to be replaced by imported stock, at great expense.

One of the most devastating hurricanes to hit Louisiana occurred in 1909. On September 20, 1909, the Grand Isle Hurricane hit Baton Rouge and New Orleans with winds up to 80 miles per hour (129 km per hour). In New Orleans, the hurricane destroyed coal barges and damaged railroads and communication lines. Practically all of the plantations between New Orleans and Baton Rouge were affected, and cotton and sugarcane crops were destroyed throughout southwest Louisiana. A 15-foot (4.6-m) storm surge flooded much of the southern part of the state. Many sailing vessels were swept ashore or sunk. Damages were estimated at $6,000,000 (the equivalent of about $2.9 billion in damages in today's dollars). The storm killed 353 people.

Today, hurricanes continue to cause destruction in Louisiana. In August 2005, Hurricane Katrina hit the Gulf Coast. Katrina was one of the five deadliest hurricanes ever to hit the United States and resulted in the deaths of more than 1,800 people. The hurricane had winds up to 175 mph (281.6 kph). These winds caused a great deal of destruction throughout the city. However, much of the damage to the city of New Orleans occurred because the levees built to hold back floodwaters from the Mississippi River failed in fifty-three places. New Orleans is built below sea level, so the failure of the city's levees had disastrous consequences. After the levees gave way, 80 percent of the city flooded. Damage from Katrina has been estimated at $81.5 billion. More than 1,577 people lost their lives in Louisiana because of the hurricane.

land. In an effort to protect cities along the coast from flood damage, people built levees to hold back the floodwaters. As a result, the land along the southern coast of Louisiana is now sinking as erosion wears away the soil.

Climate

Louisiana has a subtropical climate, with hot, humid summers and mild winters. Summer temperatures average 90 degrees Fahrenheit (32 degrees Celsius) and can reach higher than 100°F (35°C) in the southern part of the state. Average winter temperatures range from 37°F (3°C) in the northern part of the state to 46°F (8°C) in the southern region.

Plants and Animals of Louisiana

Northern Louisiana contains hickory and pine forests. Much of the land in central Louisiana is grassland prairie, suitable for farming. The southern Gulf Coast part of the state is mostly marshland, and the southwestern part of the state is prairie. The prairie is covered with various kinds of grasses and wildflowers, and has very few trees. It is dotted with wetlands and inhabited by ducks, egrets, geese, herons, and shorebirds. The prairie is also home to more than one hundred species of butterflies. Bison, red wolves, and whooping cranes once lived on the Louisiana prairies but are now extinct.

The salt marshes along the shore are populated by salt-tolerant grasses such as black rush, salt grass, saltwort, smooth cordgrass, and wire grass. The marshes are inhabited by crabs, fish, and young shrimp. They are home to a large number of bird species, including

These cypress trees grow in the backwaters of Cross Lake in Shreveport, Louisiana. Louisiana's forested wetlands contain a wide variety of wildlife.

a variety of egrets, herons, rails, terns, and other waterfowl. The bayous of Louisiana are giant swamps that contain cypress trees, Spanish moss, and live oaks (also known as evergreen oaks). They are inhabited by alligators, catfish, raccoons, water snakes, turtles, wild boar, and other small mammals. Crawfish, tiny relatives of the lobster that are a popular food in Louisiana, also live in the bayous. The state's wetlands also provide important stopover points for migrating birds.

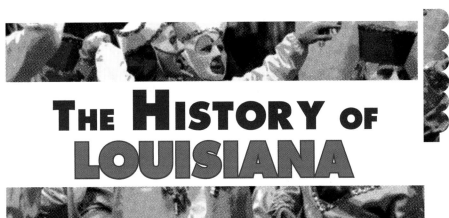

Chapter 2

THE HISTORY OF LOUISIANA

The original inhabitants of Louisiana were Native Americans. The tribes inhabiting Louisiana included the Tunica Indians in the center of the state, the Muskhogean tribes in the southeastern and east-central regions, and the Caddoan tribes in the northwest part of the state near the Red River. The Choctaw branch of the Muskhogean, who inhabited the area north of Lake Pontchartrain, were the first tribe to form an alliance with the French.

Because most of Louisiana had little large game, the majority of Native American tribes settled in permanent or temporary villages and relied on agriculture, fishing, and small game for the bulk of their food. They grew corn, beans, melons, and pumpkins. The Caddoan Indians, who lived in the far northern part of the state, also hunted buffalo on the prairies. By the time the region was colonized by Europeans in the seventeenth century, the Native American population had decreased significantly. This was due to warfare between the tribes and diseases brought to the New World by early European explorers.

Exploration

The earliest European explorer to see Louisiana was Alonso Alvarez de Pineda, who was sent by the Spanish governor of Jamaica to explore the coast of the Gulf of Mexico in 1519. Several other Spanish explorers also led expeditions through the area. One such expedition was led by Hernando de Soto, whose party traveled through the land that would become Louisiana.

The Spanish explorers who came to Louisiana were mostly interested in finding treasure. Therefore, they made no attempt to settle the land. The French were the first nation to send colonists to settle Louisiana. In fact, the state was given its name by French explorer René-Robert Cavelier, Sieur de La Salle (1643–1687), who lived in French Canada. In 1682, La Salle traveled down the Mississippi River to the Gulf of Mexico, claiming the entire Mississippi basin for France. He named the region La Louisiane ("Land of Louis") in honor of King Louis XIV, the reigning French monarch.

This painting by Thure de Thulstrup depicts La Salle taking possession of Louisiana on April 9, 1682.

Colonization

In 1698, King Louis XIV sent Pierre Le Moyne d'Iberville and his brother, Jean-Baptiste Le Moyne de Bienville, to settle Louisiana. The brothers were to bring two hundred families of colonists with them. On March 5, 1699, they arrived at what is now New Orleans. After marking their location, they traveled on to Baton Rouge. The expedition went to Lake Pontchartrain, and then continued on to Mississippi.

By the early eighteenth century, the finances of the French crown had been depleted by a series of wars. As a result, it turned control of Louisiana over to the Compagnie de la Louisiane ou d'Occident ("Company of Louisiana or the West"). This company expanded French colonization by awarding grants to people willing to establish colonies. Bienville was appointed governor of the French colony. In order to control the Mississippi River, which provided an excellent conduit for transport and trade, Bienville established his headquarters in New Orleans, which he named in honor of Philippe, duc d'Orleans, the regent who was ruling France. In 1731, the company, beset by financial problems, surrendered its charter to the government of France, and Louisiana again became a crown colony.

In 1755, the French and Indian War broke out in the New World. The British, who were allied with the Spanish, fought against the Native Americans, who had formed an alliance with the French. The war ended in 1763 when the British defeated the French, and the Treaty of Paris was signed. The Treaty of Paris gave the British control of French Canada and French lands west of the Mississippi and Florida. The French were forced to give New Orleans and all of Louisiana west of the Mississippi to Spain as a reward for helping the British win the war. The colony continued to be ruled by the Spanish until 1801.

Slavery in Louisiana

By 1719, the Louisiana colonies had begun engaging in large-scale agriculture. Cotton and sugarcane became important crops in

The Cajuns

Cajun culture plays a large role in Louisiana food, traditions, and music. But who are the Cajuns? The word "Cajun" is a corruption of the word "Acadian." In 1755, the British gained control of Nova Scotia. At this time, Nova Scotia was part of an area known as Acadia, which was made up of the Canadian Maritime Provinces Nova Scotia, New Brunswick, and Prince Edward Island. The British, who were Protestants, drove a large number of French Catholics from the area. These French Catholics, or "Acadians," fled south. Unwelcome in the other Protestant English colonies of the New World, they wound up in Louisiana in 1760. The colonial government of Louisiana settled the Cajuns in the swamps and nearby land southwest of New Orleans. By 1790, around four thousand Cajuns had settled in the bayous in southern Louisiana, where they lived by hunting and fishing. Here, Cajuns retained their culture for many years.

In the early twentieth century, laws were passed that were designed to force Cajuns to become part of mainstream society. Among these were laws forbidding the use of Cajun French in school. However, during the latter part of the century, there was a resurgence of interest in Cajun culture.

The Cajuns speak a dialect of French called "Cajun French," and more recently, "Cajun English," which incorporates Cajun pronunciation and words. Cajun cuisine is influenced by life on the bayou. It is spicy and incorporates local ingredients such as crawfish, rice, shrimp, and okra. Dishes include a spicy stew called étouffée, turtle soup, and fried alligator. They also make sausages such as spicy andouille and boudin.

Today, more than three hundred thousand descendants of Cajuns live in Louisiana. Until 2005, there were still many Cajuns living on traditional houseboats on the bayous, but Hurricane Katrina destroyed most of these. Few Cajuns still live out on the bayous, but they still make up a significant part of the population of southern Louisiana.

Louisiana by the late eighteenth century. Much of the state's agricultural work was accomplished by slave labor.

The first slaves were imported to Louisiana in the early 1700s. In 1724, Governor Bienville enacted the Black Code, a law governing the treatment of slaves. Among its rules were that slaves had to be given Catholic religious instruction and could not work on Sunday, slave families could not be broken up, slaves could buy their freedom, and they could only be punished in certain ways. When Louisiana became a state, slaves lost these protections. Under federal law, slaves had no rights and were simply considered to be the property of their owner. However, not all of the African Americans living in Louisiana were slaves. The state

This illustration is from a story by writer George Washington Cable (1844–1925). His stories depict Creole life in nineteenth-century Louisiana.

also had a considerable population of free people of color.

From 1791 to 1804, the Haitian Revolution occurred. Both slaves and free blacks rose up against French colonial rule in the Caribbean. During this period, a large number of Haitians fled the islands, settling in New Orleans. Unlike the local slave population, these people were free. They could engage in commerce and practice their own traditions, which became an important part of the culture of New Orleans and southern Louisiana. The descendants of free people of color spoke French and included a large number of affluent, skilled tradesmen and well-educated professionals. Their food, music, and religion combined elements of African, Caribbean, and French cultures. These citizens, as well as the original French settlers of New Orleans, were known as Creoles.

At this time, much of Louisiana's population was concentrated in New Orleans. As a result, Louisiana had a complicated position in regard to slavery. Because so many ships carrying imported goods entered its port, New Orleans was the largest venue for slave auctions in the country. However, because the city's economy was centered on commerce and not agriculture, Louisiana had relatively few slaves. In fact, three-quarters of African Americans in New Orleans were free. At the time of the Civil War, Louisiana had the largest population of free people of color of any state in the country, except Massachusetts.

Louisiana Becomes a State

In 1801, Napoleon Bonaparte, emperor of France, acquired Louisiana from Charles IV, the king of Spain. In 1803, U.S. president Thomas Jefferson acquired the entire French territory in the Mississippi River Basin area—reaching from Louisiana to the Canadian border—from Napoleon for $15,000,000. This block of land, known as the Louisiana Purchase, doubled the size of the United States and united the eastern and western halves of the country. On April 30, 1812, Louisiana became a state. In 1815, General Andrew Jackson defeated the British to win the Battle of New Orleans, the final battle of the War of 1812.

Louisiana in the Civil War

In the first half of the nineteenth century, there were large plantations in Louisiana that grew crops such as cotton and sugarcane. However, the economy of the state was not completely dependent on agriculture because of the growth of industry along the Mississippi River. The Mississippi was a major thoroughfare for the transport of imported goods, which arrived in the port of New Orleans and then traveled up to the Midwest and East Coast. As a result, some people in Louisiana were in favor of cooperating with the Union. Others supported the Confederacy and were in favor of secession. In 1861, Louisiana held a convention to determine the appropriate course of action. Three-quarters of the voters of New Orleans were in favor of cooperating with the Union. Nonetheless, Louisiana ultimately agreed to join the Confederacy.

At the time of the Civil War, New Orleans was the largest city in the South. Because the port of New Orleans was a key entry point for goods coming into the country, it was strategically important. Therefore, in April 1862, Union naval troops under the leadership of Admiral David Farragut (1801–1870) attacked Fort St. Philip and Fort Jackson, which guarded the mouth of the Mississippi. After defeating the forts, Farragut sailed up the Mississippi to New Orleans. Farragut occupied the city, which remained in Union control for the balance of the war. Union troops also occupied a significant portion of southern Louisiana. However, Confederate troops commanded by General Richard Taylor, the son of President Zachary Taylor, were able to keep the Union forces from taking Shreveport and the Red River Territory, and stopped the Union advance at Mansfield. Taylor's troops drove the Union forces back to Alexandria in April 1864, which ended major fighting in Louisiana.

This Currier & Ives print shows Farragut's fleet passing Fort St. Philip and Fort Jackson on the Mississippi River on April 24, 1862.

1930s and 1940s

The Great Depression was a major economic downturn caused by the collapse of banks in 1929. Millions of Americans were unemployed during this period. One of the most notable figures of the time was Huey P. Long, who was governor of Louisiana from 1928 to 1932, and senator from 1933 to 1935. He was known for his populist policies, which helped average people. For example, he instituted public works projects that provided employment to thousands of unemployed people. He supported social programs and taxation of the wealthy and corporations. However, not everyone agreed with Long's policies. He was assassinated at the state capital in 1935.

During World War II, the U.S. Army Air Force (later the U.S. Air Force) established a number of airfields in Louisiana to protect the coast from submarine attacks in the Gulf of Mexico. The airfields were also used to train fighter and bomber pilots.

The Fight for Civil Rights

In 1868, Louisiana drew up a new constitution. It granted voting and other civil rights to African American men, guaranteed African Americans access to public accommodations, and required at least one public school to be established in each parish. These schools had to admit students aged six to eighteen regardless of race. However, in practice, discrimination against African Americans continued, and after 1877, many schools again became segregated. In addition, white supremacists formed groups to terrorize black citizens fighting for civil rights. The Civil Rights Act of 1964, passed by the U.S. government, forbade discrimination against individuals on the basis of race, among other criteria.

Even after the passage of the law, there was significant conflict as African Americans attempted to exercise their right to vote and use previously segregated facilities such as restaurants. Throughout the 1950s and early 1960s, the Louisiana Legislature passed a number of bills designed to preserve segregation, even as the federal government pressed for integration. In 1953, Baton Rouge became the first southern city to engage in a boycott of segregated buses. However, in 1962, a federal court ruled that Louisiana's segregated rail and bus terminals were illegal. In 1971, the Louisiana Legislature voted, nearly unanimously, to eliminate Jim Crow laws, which made it illegal for blacks and whites to marry, dance together, or use the same restrooms, among other things. In 1989, the federal courts finally

People sit at a lunch counter at a New Orleans drugstore on September 14, 1962. For years, lunch counters, restaurants, and many other public facilities in Louisiana were segregated.

ruled that Louisiana's segregated higher education system had to be eliminated, and seventeen public colleges and universities became integrated.

By the end of the twentieth century, a commission was formed to revitalize New Orleans and promote the city as a premiere tourist destination. The commission brought together local government officials, arts groups, businesspeople, and community groups to renovate the region. After Hurricane Katrina struck in 2005, the people of the city were forced to rebuild once again. Today, New Orleans has regained two-thirds of its pre-Katrina population.

Chapter 3

THE GOVERNMENT OF LOUISIANA

Louisiana is divided into sixty-four regions, called parishes. Louisiana's parishes are like counties in other states. The government of Louisiana is divided into three parts: the executive branch, the legislative branch, and the judicial branch. The executive branch consists of the governor, lieutenant governor, and various other elected officials who are responsible for overseeing statewide programs and enforcing the laws passed by the legislature. The legislative branch's job is to pass laws. The judicial branch's job is to prosecute crimes and judge civil lawsuits.

The Executive Branch

Louisiana's governor is elected to a four-year term. The governor can only serve two consecutive terms, although he or she can run for multiple nonconsecutive terms. In addition to the governor and lieutenant governor, elected officials in the executive branch include the secretary of state, who is responsible for overseeing elections and the state archives; the attorney general, who is responsible for overseeing the prosecution of criminals; and the treasurer, who is responsible for overseeing the financial affairs of the state.

Completed in 1932, the Louisiana State Capitol in Baton Rouge is the tallest building in the city. The inset photograph shows the senate chamber inside the building during a swearing-in ceremony for new senators.

The Legislative Branch

The Louisiana Legislature consists of two houses: the senate and the house of representatives. Louisiana has 105 senators and 39 representatives. Legislators are elected to four-year terms and may not serve more than two-and-a-half consecutive terms. The legislature also approves funds for state programs and is responsible for overseeing the implementation of the programs carried out by the executive branch.

The Judicial Branch

The judicial branch has two major components: the court system, which tries those accused of crimes, and the district attorneys and law enforcement staff, who are responsible for capturing and prosecuting criminals.

There are three levels of courts in Louisiana. At the lowest level is the district court. These courts hear most criminal and civil cases. Criminal cases are those in which people accused of crimes are prosecuted by the state. Civil cases are those in which one person or organization sues another. There are forty district courts, each responsible for at least one parish.

The second level of courts is the court of appeals. If a person feels the decision made against him or her in a district court is inappropriate or unfair, he or she can apply to have the case reviewed by a court of appeals. There are five courts of appeals in Louisiana, and each is responsible for at least three district courts. Courts of appeals do not try new cases; they only review the decisions of lower courts.

The highest state court is the supreme court. The supreme court reviews the decisions of the lower courts. It decides cases in

The Napoleonic Code

The laws governing Louisiana were first written down and published in the Civil Code Digest of 1808 and printed in both English and French. The Civil Code was based on the system of French civil law established under Emperor Napoleon in 1804, which in turn, was based on Roman law.

Often referred to as the "Napoleonic Code," the French system of law is based on written laws that specifically spell out what is illegal. The states formed from the English colonies adopted English common law, which is based on precedent. This means that the law is built on decisions made in the past. Under the English system of law, the law is shaped by prior court decisions. Under the French system, the judge is free to interpret the law as he or she sees fit, without regard to how previous judges have interpreted it. Since Louisiana was settled by French colonists, the state adopted the French system of civil law.

Today, all the other states in the country, including those that were formed from previously French territory, use the English system of common law. This means that lawyers who move to Louisiana from other states, or move from Louisiana to other states, must learn a new system of law. No other state practices the same system of civil law that Louisiana does.

Unlike many states, when people marry in Louisiana, the property they've acquired automatically belongs to both spouses. Inheritance laws are also different in Louisiana. They are designed to keep land in families. In most states, if a married person dies without a will, his or her spouse will inherit all property, including real estate. However, in Louisiana, unless the spouse paid for part of the property, preference is given to the deceased person's closest family members, such as children or parents.

which there is a question regarding the proper application of laws; when the law under which a person has been convicted is declared unconstitutional by the federal Supreme Court; or when the death penalty has been imposed on a convicted person. The supreme court has a chief justice and six associate justices, who are all elected for ten-year terms.

In addition to justices serving in the courts, there are a variety of personnel who are involved in the capture of criminals. In each parish, a sheriff is elected for four years. There are also district attorneys, or lawyers who prosecute defendants. Clerks of the court are elected to four-year terms and are responsible for processing legal documents and maintaining court records.

The Louisiana State Supreme Court is in New Orleans. Outside the building is a statue of Edward Douglass White, the only Louisianan to serve on the U.S. Supreme Court.

Chapter 4

THE ECONOMY OF LOUISIANA

One of the major industries in Louisiana is tourism, much of which is centered on New Orleans. Louisiana also has a significant agricultural industry. Louisiana is the second largest producer of petroleum and the third largest producer of natural gas in the country. The transportation of goods entering the country through the Gulf of Mexico has been important to Louisiana's economy since the area was first settled. Louisiana has a number of major ports through which goods enter the United States. The largest is New Orleans, which is the eighth largest port in the world.

Tourism and Entertainment

Louisiana is known for its unique Creole and Cajun cuisine. New Orleans, in particular, is famed for its restaurants and celebrity chefs. Another well-known draw for tourists is music. New Orleans has long been famous for jazz, and the clubs in the city's French Quarter neighborhood have played host to many of the world's most famous jazz musicians. Today, the clubs still flourish, offering a wide range of musical styles.

The French Quarter itself—also known as the Vieux Carré ("Old Square")—is lined with many quaint old buildings and shops that sell antiques and crafts. Throughout Louisiana, there are a number of plantations that are open to visitors, where one can tour the main house and grounds to get a feel for what it was like to live in Louisiana years ago. In addition, people can view the state's wildlife in a variety of bayou tours and in the state's many natural recreation areas.

Louisiana is also closely associated with the supernatural. New Orleans boasts a number of picturesque old cemeteries with ornate white crypts. These crypts had to be built aboveground because it was not possible to bury people in the marshy soil. Many companies offer ghost and cemetery tours of the city.

A carriage passes through New Orleans' French Quarter. A popular tourist attraction, the French Quarter is the oldest neighborhood in the city.

Louisiana is famously linked to the practice of voodoo. Voodoo was a religion practiced by many of the Haitians who settled in New Orleans. Many people still practice voodoo today. Voodoo is marketed to tourists in a variety of ways, from shops selling voodoo charms to the Voodoo Museum in the original home of Marie Laveau, a legendary practitioner of the religion.

Mardi Gras

One of the biggest events in Louisiana is the annual Mardi Gras celebration. Although parades and balls take place throughout the state, Mardi Gras is most closely associated with New Orleans, where it draws tourists from all over the world. Mardi Gras literally means "Fat Tuesday." It is a name given to a series of celebrations that lead up to Ash Wednesday, the day that marks the beginning of the period of Lent in the Catholic religion. During Lent people are supposed to give up certain luxuries. Traditionally, many Catholics did not eat meat during this period. Thus, "Fat Tuesday" was a day of feasting marked by the slaughter of a fatted bull.

Mardi Gras has been celebrated in New Orleans since 1743, when the governor of Louisiana, Pierre François de Rigaud, Marquis de Vaudreuil, established balls and banquets for the upper class. Some celebrants strolled or rode through the city by foot, horse, or carriage, showing off their finery. However, the first real Mardi Gras parade did not take place in New Orleans until 1837. The revelers were so rowdy that the parades were almost banned.

In 1857, six prominent members of New Orleans society formed the first krewe, Comus. Krewes are secret social organizations that each mount a Mardi Gras parade around a specific theme. In the nineteenth century, parades lit by torches took place at night. They featured floats that were constructed and decorated by the krewes. The members of the original nineteenth-century krewes wore masks to hide their identities as they rode on the floats, and each elected a king who presided over a costume ball. Those on the floats tossed trinkets and beads to people they knew among the watchers. Mardi Gras parades were banned during the Civil War but returned afterward.

Today, Mardi Gras parades feature elaborate floats, many containing moving figures and fiber-optic lights. Collecting beads and other "throws" has become a major goal of tourists, so the costumed riders on floats toss vast quantities of these souvenirs to the crowds. Among the most coveted are Mardi Gras doubloons, aluminum coins stamped with symbols of the krewes.

Louisiana's two professional sports teams are both based in New Orleans. They are the New Orleans Hornets basketball team and the New Orleans Saints football team. The Saints play at the famous Superdome in downtown New Orleans. In addition, the state is home to a wide range of college sports teams.

This worker harvests sugarcane on a farm near Franklin, Louisiana. One of Louisiana's chief agricultural products, sugarcane is very important to the economy of the state.

Agriculture

Forestry is the largest agricultural industry in the state, which has 13.9 million acres (5.63 million hectares) of forest. Cotton, rice, soybeans, sugarcane, and sweet potatoes are grown in Louisiana. Louisiana is the second largest producer of sugarcane and sweet potatoes in the United States and the third largest grower of rice. The state is the major producer of the tabasco pepper, which is used to make Tabasco sauce.

Louisiana supplies 25 percent of the seafood produced in the United States. It ranks number one in the nation in the production of alligators, crawfish, oysters, and shrimp. Louisiana is a major supplier of crabs, catfish, and a number of other fish. In addition, the state produces poultry and dairy products.

Ships from Africa, Asia, Europe, Latin America, and the United States bring in cargo to the port of New Orleans. These ships are passing through the port's Industrial Canal.

Energy

According to the Louisiana Mid-Continent Oil and Gas Association, the state's first oil well was built in 1901 in Jennings Field. Oil was first collected off the Louisiana coast in 1947. There are nineteen refineries in Louisiana that process oil into commodities like gasoline. Two of the United States' Strategic Petroleum Reserve facilities are located in Louisiana. These reserves protect the United States in the event that there is a disruption in the importation of oil into the country. According to the U.S. Department of Energy, the Louisiana Offshore Oil Port is the only port in the United States that is capable of accommodating deep-draft oil tankers. These are ships whose oil tanks extend far below the waterline.

Shipping

Coffee, rubber, steel, and manufactured goods enter the port of New Orleans by ship and are dispersed throughout the nation by truck, as well as by six railway lines that serve the port. Commodities such as grain are also transported by barge up the Mississippi River to the interior of the country. More than 40 percent of grain shipments from the United States and 25 percent of the country's exports that are carried by ships move through Louisiana's ports.

Chapter 5

PEOPLE FROM LOUISIANA:
PAST AND PRESENT

Louisiana has a long and fascinating history. Many famous Louisianans are most closely associated with the arts. With its rich heritage and mix of cultures, the state provides fertile ground for actors, musicians, singers, and writers. Louisiana was also the first state to have an African American governor. The following are some notable people from Louisiana who have had a significant role in the arts, politics, the military, and science.

P. G. T. Beauregard (1818–1893) Born on a sugarcane plantation about 20 miles (32 km) from New Orleans, Beauregard was a Confederate Civil War general at Fort Sumter in Charleston, South Carolina, at the start of the war. He commanded Confederate troops at the First Battle of Bull Run in Virginia in 1861; the Battle of Shiloh in Tennessee in 1862; and the Siege of Corinth in Mississippi in 1862, among others.

Ruth R. Benerito (1916–) Born and raised in New Orleans, Benerito is a scientist in the textile industry who invented wrinkle-free cotton for "permanent press" clothing.

After earning a Ph.D. in physical chemistry, she went to work for the U.S. Department of Agriculture's Southern Regional Research Center in New Orleans. Her research also led to the development of flame- and stain-resistant fabrics.

Michael DeBakey (1908–2008) Born in Lake Charles, Louisiana, DeBakey was the inventor of the artificial heart. While still in medical school at Tulane University, he invented a type of pump that is now used in heart-lung machines during heart surgery. He was also one of the first doctors to perform cardiac bypass surgery, in which arteries in the heart are replaced, and pioneered other medical procedures.

Michael DeBakey performed the operation to implant the first artificial heart. He earned many awards for his contributions to medicine.

Ellen DeGeneres (1958–) Born in Metairie, Louisiana, DeGeneres began her career as a stand-up comedian and went on to become an actress and the host of *The Ellen DeGeneres Show*. She was the voice of Dory in the 2003 movie *Finding Nemo*.

New Orleans Music

Jazz music has always been an important part of Louisiana's culture. Jazz has its roots in the eighteenth- and nineteenth-century African and Caribbean music of Louisiana's black population. The music was also influenced by popular forms of American music at the time, such as ragtime.

New Orleans has produced many outstanding jazz musicians, including Sidney Bechet, Ellis and Wynton Marsalis, Jelly Roll Morton, Nicholas Payton, and many others. Perhaps the most famous jazz great to emerge from Louisiana is Louis Armstrong (1901–1971). Armstrong's experience as an early jazz musician in the state was similar to that of his contemporaries. Born in New Orleans, Armstrong became famous as a trumpet player and singer. He left school at age eleven and joined a group of other boys playing music on the streets. Bunk Johnson, a cornet player, taught Armstrong to play by ear. At fourteen, Armstrong got his first professional job, playing at a music hall. Then he played in brass bands on the riverboats on the Mississippi. In the early 1920s, he moved to Chicago to join musician King Oliver's band. King Oliver was one of Armstrong's mentors in New Orleans. In Chicago, he began to make recordings and acquire a national reputation. Ultimately, Armstrong became one of the world's most well-known and respected jazz musicians.

Today, New Orleans is still home to many jazz bands. Traditional New Orleans jazz is still very much a part of the culture of the city. The Preservation Hall Jazz Band continues to play classic New Orleans jazz and ragtime for adoring audiences. The city's traditional brass bands, which played in parades at funerals and Mardi Gras, have been revitalized by a new generation of musicians who have blended traditional jazz with modern styles such as hip-hop, funk, and reggae. New Orleans has also produced a number of well-known hip-hop artists, including Lil' Wayne, Master P, and Mystikal.

Oscar James Dunn (c. 1826–1871) Born in New Orleans, Dunn was lieutenant governor of Louisiana and the first African American governor of any U.S. state. Elected in 1868, he served until his death in 1877. Dunn was succeeded by state senator P. B. S. Pinchback, another African American politician, who served as acting governor of the state for thirty-four days upon the death of the governor.

David Filo (1966–) David Filo moved to Moss Bluff, Louisiana, at age six. Filo is the cofounder, along with Jerry Yang, of the technology company Yahoo!. He met Yang while they were both attending Stanford University. Filo wrote the original software that allowed the Yahoo! search engine to function.

Entertainer Randy Jackson is the producer of the TV show *America's Best Dance Crew* on MTV and is a judge on *American Idol.*

Randy Jackson (1956–) Born in Baton Rouge, Jackson is a singer, musician, and record producer. He performed with the rock band Journey, and was musical director for a number of Mariah Carey's tours. Jackson was a vice president of

Columbia Records and head of MCA Records for four years. Jackson is a judge on the TV show *American Idol*.

Elmore Leonard (1925–) Born in New Orleans, Leonard is a novelist and screenwriter. He began his career in the 1950s writing westerns, but he is best known for his crime fiction. Many of his books have been made into movies, including *Get Shorty*, *3:10 to Yuma*, and *Mr. Majestyk*, among others.

Anne Rice (1941–) A native of New Orleans, Rice is the author of many supernatural and horror novels. Her most famous works are her many vampire novels, beginning with *Interview with the Vampire* in 1976. Almost one hundred million copies of her books have been sold around the world.

Louis Charles Roudanez (1823–1890) A free-born African American, Roudanez was raised in New Orleans, and studied medicine in Paris and at Dartmouth College in New Hampshire. He founded the first African American daily newspaper, the *New Orleans Tribune*, in 1864. The *Tribune* was dedicated to social justice for African Americans.

Madam C. J. Walker (1867–1919) Born Sarah Breedlove in Delta, Louisiana, Madam C. J. Walker was a famous businesswoman. She created the Madam C. J. Walker Manufacturing Company, which produced a hugely successful line of hair care products for African American women. Walker is cited

This circa-1914 portrait shows Madame C. J. Walker, the first self-made woman millionaire. She left two-thirds of her estate to charitable organizations when she died, including the NAACP.

in the *Guinness Book of World Records* as the first self-made woman entrepreneur to become a millionaire.

Reese Witherspoon (1976–) Born in New Orleans, Witherspoon is an actress whose films include *Legally Blonde*, *Sweet Home Alabama*, and *Walk the Line*. She earned an Oscar, Golden Globe, and Screen Actors Guild award for her role as June Carter Cash in *Walk the Line*.

Timeline

1673	Louis Joliet and Pere Marquette explore the Mississippi River.
1682	La Salle claims the land along the Mississippi River for France.
1699	Pierre Le Moyne d'Iberville lands at the sites of present-day New Orleans and Baton Rouge.
1717	The Compagnie de la Louisiane ou d'Occident takes control of Louisiana.
1724	Governor Bienville enacts the Black Code.
1731	Louisiana becomes a crown colony again.
1762	At the conclusion of the French and Indian War, France is forced by Britain to turn Louisiana over to Spain.
1791–1804	The Haitian Revolution occurs.
1801	Emperor Napoleon of France acquires Louisiana from Spain.
1803	The Louisiana Purchase occurs.
1812	Louisiana becomes the eighteenth state.
1815	The Battle of New Orleans, the last battle of the War of 1812, takes place.
1861	Louisiana secedes from the Union and becomes part of the Confederacy.
1862	Union Admiral David Farragut occupies New Orleans.
1868	Louisiana is readmitted to the Union.
1879	Captain James B. Eads constructs the first jetty system at the port of New Orleans to keep the mouth of the Mississippi River from silting up.
1928	Huey P. Long is elected governor.
1964	The Civil Rights Act of 1964 outlaws racial discrimination.
1971	Jim Crow laws supporting segregation are repealed.
1975	The New Orleans Superdome is constructed.
2005	Hurricane Katrina devastates New Orleans and the Gulf Coast.
2010	The New Orleans Saints win the Super Bowl for the first time.

State motto:	"Union, Justice & Confidence"
State capital:	Baton Rouge
State fruit:	Strawberry
State flower:	Magnolia (white)
State bird:	Brown pelican
State tree:	Bald cypress
State dog:	Catahoula leopard dog
Statehood date and number:	April 30, 1812; eighteenth state
State nickname:	The Pelican State
Total area and U.S. rank:	51,843 square miles (134,272.75 square km); thirty-first largest state
Population:	4.4 million
Length of coastline:	397 miles (639 km)

State Flag

State Seal

Highest elevation:	Driskill Mountain, at 535 feet (165 m)
Lowest elevation:	New Orleans, at 5 feet (1.5 m) below sea level
Major rivers:	Atchafalaya River, Mississippi River, Ouachita River, Red River, Sabine River
Major lakes:	Catahoula Lake, Grand Lake, Lake Charles, Lake Maurepas, Lake Pontchartrain, Toledo Bend Reservoir, White Lake
Hottest recorded temperature:	114°F (45.56°C), August 10, 1936, at Plain Dealing
Coldest recorded temperature:	–16°F (–26.67°C), February 13, 1899, at Minden
Origin of state name:	Named for King Louis XIV of France
Chief agricultural products:	Chickens, cotton, rice, sweet potatoes, sugarcane, wood
Major industries:	Agriculture, oil and natural gas, seafood, shipping, tourism

Brown pelican

Magnolia

GLOSSARY

amphibious Capable of existing on both land and sea.

antebellum The era prior to the Civil War.

bayou A swamp.

conduit A pipeline.

crescent A shape resembling a quarter moon.

delinquency Acts of illegal or antisocial behavior, usually committed by a minor.

deposit A layer of sediment that has turned into rock.

erosion The wearing away of a substance.

extinct No longer in existence.

judicial Related to justice, or to the court system.

legislative Having to do with the law.

levee An embankment or wall created to hold back water.

music hall A theater where variety shows are performed.

parish In Louisiana, a parish is the equivalent of a county in other states.

petroleum Unrefined oil.

pivotal Playing a central role.

prosecute To attempt to prove someone guilty of a crime.

regent Someone who rules a country in place of a king or queen who is too young to rule, or unable to rule.

reveler A person who is celebrating something.

sediment Soil and minerals that sink to the bottom of a body of water.

Blaine Kern's Mardi Gras World

1380 Port of New Orleans Place

New Orleans, LA 70130

(504) 362-8213

Web site: http://www.mardigrasworld.com

Blaine Kern Studios builds many of the Mardi Gras floats used in the major parades. The company provides tours of facilities, where participants can see workers making floats and the props used in past floats.

The Cabildo

701 Chartres Street

New Orleans, LA

(504) 568-6968

Web site: http://lsm.crt.state.la.us/cabex.htm

The seat of the colonial Spanish government and site of the Louisiana Purchase, the Cabildo is now a museum detailing Louisiana history.

Coushatta Tribe of Louisiana

P.O. Box 8181

Elton, LA 0532

(318) 992-2717

Web site: http://www.coushattatribela.org

The Coushatta tribe maintains a museum and offers tours of the reservation.

Louisiana Department of Wildlife and Fisheries

2000 Quail Drive

Baton Rouge, LA 70808

(225) 765-2800

Web site: http://www.wlf.louisiana.gov

This organization provides information on the wildlife of Louisiana, including conservation efforts.

Louisiana State Museum

660 N. 4th Street

Baton Rouge, LA 70802

(225) 342-5428

Web site: http://lsm.crt.state.la.us/BR/br.htm

This museum features diverse exhibits on Louisiana's history, industry, and culture.

National World War II Museum

945 Magazine Street

New Orleans, LA 70130

(504) 527-6012

Web site: http://www.ddaymuseum.org

This museum provides permanent and special exhibits on World War II.

New Orleans Historic Voodoo Museum

724 Dumaine Street

New Orleans, LA 70116

(504) 680-0128

Web site: http://www.voodoomuseum.com

This museum covers the history and folklore of voodoo.

Oak Alley Plantation

3645 Highway 18

Vacherie, LA 70090

(225) 265-2151

Web site: http://www.oakalleyplantation.com

Visitors can tour the house and grounds of this antebellum plantation located between New Orleans and Baton Rouge.

Web Sites

Due to the changing nature of Internet links, Rosen Publishing has developed an online list of Web sites related to the subject of this book. This site is updated regularly. Please use this link to access the list:

http://www.rosenlinks.com/uspp/lapp

Allured, Janet, and Judith F. Gentry, ed. *Louisiana Women: Their Lives and Times*. Athens, GA: University of Georgia Press, 2009.

Aloian, Molly. *Mardi Gras and Carnival*. New York, NY: Crabtree Press, 2009.

Burgin, Michael. *The Louisiana Purchase*. Chicago, IL: Heinemann-Raintree, 2007.

DK Publishing. *Civil War Battles and Leaders*. New York, NY: DK Publishing, 2004.

Elish, Dan. *Louis Armstrong and the Jazz Age*. Danbury, CT: Children's Press, 2008.

Gross, Steve, and Sue Daley. *Creole Houses: Traditional Homes of Old Louisiana*. New York, NY: Abrams, 2007.

Holt, Kimberly Willis. *Part of Me: Stories of a Louisiana Family*. New York, NY: Macmillan/Square Fish: 2005.

Kent, Deborah. *The Great Mississippi Flood of 1927*. Danbury, CT: Children's Press, 2009.

Lachoff, Irwin, and Catherine C. Kahn. *The Jewish Community of New Orleans*. Chicago, IL: Arcadia Publishing, 2005.

Landau, Elaine. *The Civil Rights Movement in America*. Danbury, CT: Children's Press, 2007.

Macaulay, Ellen. *Louisiana*. Danbury, CT: Children's Press, 2009.

MacBride, Roger Lea. *On the Banks of the Bayou*. New York, NY: HarperCollins, 1998.

Miller, Deborah. *Hurricane Katrina: Devastation on the Gulf Coast*. San Diego, CA: Lucent Books, 2006.

Rodrigue, Sylvia Frank, and Faye Phillips. *Baton Rouge*. Chicago, IL: Arcadia Publishing, 2008.

Roland, Gwen. *Atchafalaya Houseboat: My Years in the Louisiana Swamp*. Baton Rouge, LA: Louisiana State University Press, 2006.

Strom, Laura Layton. *Built Below Sea Level: New Orleans*. Danbury, CT: Children's Press, 2007.

Stuart, Bonnye F. *More Than Petticoats: Remarkable Louisiana Women*. Guilford, CT: Morris Book Publishing, 2009.

Torres, John Albert. *Hurricane Katrina and the Devastation of New Orleans, 2005*. Hockessin, DE: Mitchell Lane Publishers, 2006.

Zum, Jon. *The Louisiana Purchase*. Edina, MN: ABDO Publishing, 2007.

BIBLIOGRAPHY

Bauman, Harriet. "French Creoles in New Orleans." Yale University Yale-New Haven Teachers Institute. Retrieved, October 2, 2009 (http://www.yale.edu/ynhti/curriculum/units/1992/2/92.02.02.x.html).

Calhoun, Milburn, ed. *Louisiana Almanac 2006–2007*. Gretna, LA: Pelican Publishing, 2006.

Duluth News Tribune. "Louisiana and Mississippi Grand Isle Hurricane, September 1909." Transcribed by Linda Horton on May 27, 2008. Retrieved September 15, 2009 (http://www3.gendisasters.com/louisiana/6552/louisiana-mississippi-hurricane-sept-1909).

International Council on Monuments and Sites. "New Orleans, Hurricane Katrina, and Global Climate Change." *ICOMOS World Report 2006/2007 on Monuments and Sites in Danger*. Retrieved August 24, 2009 (http://www.international.icomos.org/risk/world_report/2006-2007/pdf/H@R_2006-2007_60_Special_Focus_New_Orleans_Katrina.pdf).

Johnson, Jerah. "Jim Crow Laws of the 1890s and the Origins of New Orleans Jazz: Correction of an Error." *Popular Music*, 19:2, Cambridge University Press, 2000, pp. 243–251. Retrieved September 20, 2009 (http://journals.cambridge.org/action/displayAbstract;jsessionid=97608A99CF1A69A3B19D2EAACB9CD175.tomcat1?fromPage=online&aid=61752).

Karnow, Stanley. "My Debt to Cousin Louis's Coronet." *New York Times*, February 21, 2001. Retrieved October 8, 2009 (http://www.nytimes.com/2001/02/21/opinion/my-debt-to-cousin-louis-s-cornet.html?sec=health).

Louisiana Department of Wildlife and Fisheries. "Louisiana's Cajun Prairie: An Endangered Ecosystem." Retrieved September 16, 2009 (http://www.wlf.louisiana.gov/pdfs/lacons/lacp.pdf).

Louisiana Geological Survey. "The Geology of Louisiana." Retrieved August 24, 2009 (http://www.lgs.lsu.edu/deploy/uploads/gengeotext.pdf).

Louisiana.gov. "Government." Retrieved September 24, 2009 (http://www.louisiana.gov/Government).

Louisiana State Museum. "Reconstruction: A State Divided." Retrieved October 3, 2009 (http://lsm.crt.state.la.us/cabildo/cab11.htm).

National Park Service. "A Brief History of New Orleans Jazz." Retrieved October 8, 2009 (http://www.nps.gov/archive/jazz/Jazz%20History_origins_pre1895.htm).

New Orleans Online. "Port of New Orleans." Retrieved October 3, 2009 (http://www.neworleansonline.com/neworleans/business/port.html).

Nutria.com. "Nutria in Louisiana." Retrieved September 16, 2009 (http://www.nutria.com/uploads/0232.brochurerev.pdf).

Social Security Administration. "Social Security History: Huey P. Long's Speeches." Retrieved October 2, 2009 (http://www.ssa.gov/history/longsen.html).

TheCajuns.com. "Hurricanes in Louisiana History." Retrieved October 4, 2009 (http://www.thecajuns.com/lahurricanes.htm).

U.S. Department of Agriculture/Louisiana Agriculture in the Classroom. "A Look at Louisiana Agriculture." Retrieved October 2, 2009 (http://www.agclassroom.org/kids/stats/louisiana.pdf).

Wall, Bennett H., Light Townsend Cummins, Judith Kelleher Schafer, Edward F. Haas, and Michael L. Kurtz. *Louisiana: A History*. Wheeling, IL: Harlan-Davidson, 2008.

About the Author

Jeri Freedman has a bachelor of arts degree from Harvard University. She is the author of more than thirty young adult nonfiction books, including *Massachusetts: Past and Present* and *Iowa: Past and Present*. She is also the coauthor of two alternate history science fiction novels published under the name Ellen Foxxe. She splits her time between her homes in New Orleans and Boston.

Photo Credits